Riches of the Earth

Oil

Irene Franck and David Brownstone

GROLIER

An imprint of Scholastic Library Publishing
Danbury, Connecticut

Credits and Acknowledgments

abbreviations: t (top), b (bottom), l (left), r (right), c (center)

Image credits: Art Resource: 12 (Giraudon), 14; Bethlehem Steel Corporation: 22; CORBIS: 9 (Michael T. Sedam); Getty Images/PhotoDisc: 5b (PhotoLink); National Aeronautics and Space Administration (NASA): 1t and running heads; Photo Researchers, Inc.: 3 (Paolo Koch), 8 (Tom Hollyman), 13 (Lowell Georgia), 25 (Richard R. Hansen), 27b (Wesley Bocxe), 28 (Gary Retherford); Photo Researchers, Inc./Science Photo Library: 1b and 5t (detail) (Astrid and Hans Frieder Michler), 21 (Martin Bond), 23 (Pekka Parviainen); U.S. Coast Guard: 17 (PA2 Chad Saylor), 24; U.S. Department of Defense: 29; U.S. Department of Energy: 19, 20l, 20r, 26; Woodfin Camp & Associates: 4 (P. Boulat/Cosmos); 6, 18, and 27t (Chuck Nacke); 7 (A. Ramey), 10 (Dick Durrance), 11 and 15 (Robert Azzi). Original image drawn for this book by K & P Publishing Services: 16.

Our thanks to Joe Hollander, Phil Friedman, and Laurie McCurley at Scholastic Library Publishing; to photo researchers Susan Hormuth, Robin Sand, and Robert Melcak; to copy editor Michael Burke; and to the librarians throughout the northeastern library network, in particular to the staff of the Chappaqua Library—director Mark Hasskarl; the expert reference staff, including Martha Alcott, Michele J. Capozzella, Maryanne Eaton, Catherine Paulsen, Jane Peyraud, Paula Peyraud, and Carolyn Reznick; and the circulation staff, headed by Barbara Le Sauvage—for fulfilling our wide-ranging research needs.

Published 2003 by Grolier
Division of Scholastic Library Publishing
Old Sherman Turnpike
Danbury, Connecticut 06816

For information address the publisher:
Scholastic Library Publishing, Grolier Division
Old Sherman Turnpike, Danbury, Connecticut 06816

© 2003 Irene M. Franck and David M. Brownstone

Library of Congress Cataloging-in-Publication Data

Franck, Irene M.
    Oil / Irene Franck and David Brownstone.
      p. cm. -- (Riches of the earth ; v. 6)
    Summary: Provides information about oil and its importance in everyday life.
    Includes bibliographical references and index.
    ISBN 0-7172-5730-4 (set : alk. paper) -- ISBN 0-7172-5718-5 (vol. 6 : alk paper)
    1. Petroleum--Juvenile literature [1. Petroleum.]2. Petroleum industry and trade.] I. Brownstone, David M. II. Title.

TN870.3.F73 2003
553.2'82--dc21

2003044082

Printed in the United States of America

Designed by K & P Publishing Services

Contents

Oil—Disappearing Treasure

Oil fields around the world are often marked by burning gas flares like these in modern Libya. That is because pockets of natural gas are often found near oil deposits. The gas may be burned off to avoid explosions, or it can be captured for use as a fuel itself.

Oil (petroleum) is by far the most important of humanity's fuels. It is the main fuel that heats our homes, offices, schools, and industrial plants. As gasoline, it is the fuel that powers our automobiles, trucks, motorcycles, airplanes, tanks, ships, and other vehicles.

Oil is also much more, for it is the basic substance used to lubricate our machines, make asphalt for our roads, and create literally thousands of other oil-based products. In addition, many chemicals, called *petrochemicals* (see p. 5), are made from oil. These, in turn, are used to

Petroleum and Petrochemicals

The more formal name for oil is *petroleum*. This name explains its origin, for it means "oil" (*-leum*) from "rock" (*petro-*). That's why many modern products made from oil are called *petrochemicals*.

Humans use many other kinds of oils, such as olive oil or corn oil in cooking. Even so, most people still call petroleum simply *oil*.

create thousands of other products, including plastics, soaps, fertilizers, glues, and synthetic (human-made) materials of all sorts—flooring and carpet materials, polyester clothing, recording discs and tapes, even nylon basketball uniforms and soccer balls!

Only a century ago the worldwide supply of oil seemed limitless. People thought they only had to find it and take it out of the ground. However, it turns out that the world's oil supply is far from limitless.

That is partly due to population growth. In 1900 the world held 2 billion people, but now there are 6 billion of us. Within the 21st century there will probably be 12 billion people on Earth—with a total appetite for oil that could hardly have been imagined in 1900.

If you play soccer, chances are your shoes or the soccer ball itself are made from petrochemicals, substances that come from oil.

Not only are there far more people using oil and its products, but now there are also many more ways of using oil than there were back in 1900.

Oil has largely replaced coal, formerly the main fuel used as a source of heat. For many people all over the world, oil has also replaced wood as a heating source, as that widely used fuel has become much harder to find and far more expensive than ever before.

The plain fact is that oil is a *declining resource*, meaning that the worldwide supply of oil is being used up—and there is no known way of creating more of it. New supplies of oil, some of them large, continue to be found in several parts of the world. Even so, the world's oil will all too soon be gone.

Some geologists feel that the world's oil will last as long as 200 years, but many believe it will last only another 50 to 75 years. In any event, humanity will have to find other ways of doing all the things oil does for us now—and there is no time to be wasted.

In the meantime, however, oil remains one of the most valuable substances in the world. It is sought—and all too often fought over—by all the world's peoples. Because oil is so important as an energy source, finding and protecting oil resources has become a major source of international conflict.

The fuel needed to run all our cars, trucks, tractors, motorcycles, jets, tanks, ships, and most other kinds of motorized vehicles comes from oil.

Oil under the ground is a liquid, but when it is spilled in cool ocean waters, it becomes a sticky, gooey mass. That is what happened to this oil, spilled from a tanker onto a beach in California.

What Is Oil?

Oil is a kind of liquid fuel. When it burns, it provides heat to keep us warm, light to brighten our darkness, and power to run everything from the family car to a huge industry.

Oil is called a *fossil fuel* because it is composed of plant matter that decayed long, long ago. A pool of oil buried deep in the earth may have started its life tens of millions of years ago as a huge, dense, color-ful tropical forest teeming with dinosaurs, immense trees, and thousands of kinds of plants and animals now long extinct. Over the course of many millions of years, the forest's plant matter died, de-cayed, and finally was buried under layers of *sediment*—that is, earth and other natural materials that settled to the bottom of a body of water, such as a flowing stream.

Oil

Eventually, over many more millions of years, the layers of sediment turned into solid rock, trapping the plant matter under it. Over time these pools of plant matter, trapped in several kinds of rock formations and subjected to great pressure and heat, changed into pools of oil.

Those pools of oil—some as little as 50 feet across and some far larger—are the reservoirs of oil that people drill into today. Very often such oil pools have layers of natural gas trapped on top of them and large pools of water trapped below them.

Oil as it comes out of the ground is called *crude oil*. It is composed mainly of *hydrocarbons*, a group of chemical compounds (mixed materials) containing hydrogen and carbon, along with other compounds containing oxygen, nitrogen, and sulfur. These chemical compounds differ widely, depending on such matters as what chemicals they contain, how deep they are buried, and under what physical conditions they were formed.

There are several kinds of crude oils, colored from amber to black and including many shades of brown and green. Crude oils also contain different amounts of sulfur,

Oil comes in many thicknesses and colors, like these oil samples at an oil storage facility in New Jersey.

heavy metals, and salts. Oils also vary as to how freely they flow (primarily a matter of their thickness, called *viscosity*), the temperature at which they can be poured (called the *pour point*), and their weight (*specific gravity*).

Oil that contains large amounts of sulfur is called *sour crude*. The sulfur and crude oil interact to create the chemical hydrogen sulfide, which has a terrible smell. Sour crude can also damage machinery, including oil refinery machinery. Because of that, sour crude is "sweetened" by removing much of the sulfur in desulfurization plants before it is refined.

Quantities of oil are usually measured in *barrels*. This is a measure of volume, not weight, since different crude oils have different weights. By common practice, one barrel of oil contains about 42 gallons of oil. However, barrels of other sizes are sometimes used.

A single oil well may yield as little as 15 to 20 barrels of oil in a day—or an enormous 100,000 barrels a day. A few wells have even produced more than 200,000 barrels a day.

Oil is generally measured in barrels. These vary in volume but are roughly the size of the barrels stacked up in this Alaska oil storage facility.

Other Fossil Fuels

Oil shale is a kind of rock that contains large quantities of a kind of heavy oil much like petroleum. Geologists and chemists do not consider it to be actually a kind of petroleum. However, in the long run oil shale may meet many needs of an oil-hungry world.

Tar sands are a kind of sand containing a very heavy sort of oil. It may also come to supply large amounts of oil to the world. For technical reasons this kind of oil is very difficult and expensive to separate out from the sands. However, those technical problems may be solved in the future.

Coal is another major fossil fuel, but this one is a solid rather than a liquid. Like oil, coal is a declining resource. There is far more coal left in the ground than there is oil. Yet it would be very difficult to adapt coal to all of oil's many uses. Coal is also, perhaps even more than oil, damaging to the environment.

Oil shale contains a kind of oil similar to petroleum. This area of oil shale in Colorado has caught fire and is burning.

Oil was used for some thousands of years, where it seeped up naturally from underground pools, as here in the modern Saudi Arabian desert. However, the amounts found and used were tiny compared to those used today.

Oil in History

Oil has been known and used by people for thousands of years. Yet it has been a major factor in human history only since the early 1900s. Indeed, the oddest thing about oil is that, because it is running out, it is likely to be important for only a short time in the history of humanity.

A thick, heavy form of oil called *asphalt* was known and used for at least 5,000 years in ancient Sumeria and later in Babylonia (both in what is now Iraq). By at least 3,000 years ago asphalt was also being used in Mexico. However, most oil was found at the surface in the form of seepage from underground pools, as occurred throughout the Middle East in ancient times.

In Egypt and several other countries, oil from seepage was used as a medicine and to relieve skin ailments, such as burns and sores. Oil continued to be used for medicinal purposes throughout the world, including the Americas.

Oil was also used for religious purposes. At Baku, now part of a great oil-producing area in the Caucasus Mountains region (shared by Russia and several neighboring countries), oil seepage from underground pools was sometimes set afire naturally (as by lightning) or by people. Some of the resulting fires would become a set of "eternal flames," at which thousands came to worship every year.

From ancient times into the modern era, burning, oil-soaked arrows or barrels were also used to set fire to enemy forts and settlements. Warfare at sea saw oil used to create a "flaming sea," aimed at setting fire to enemy ships.

Eventually people began digging wells in the ground to get more oil. There were wells producing oil in the eastern Mediterranean more than 2,000 years ago and in Southeast Asia by at least 1,000 years ago. The Chinese had natural gas wells 800 years ago (by around 1200 A.D.), and some reports indicate that they were also producing oil from wells at that time. How-

For centuries soldiers would shoot oil-soaked arrows or barrels at an enemy's fort, trying to set it on fire. This is a 17th-century "war machine" designed for shooting a burning barrel.

This is the site of the oil well drilled in Titusville, Pennsylvania, in 1859 by Edwin L. Drake. Many people see it as the birthplace of the modern oil industry.

ever, the amounts of oil produced by such wells were very small.

Modern Times

By the 1800s whale oil was being widely burned in lamps in the United States and several other countries as a lighting source. However, by then whales were becoming scarce due to overhunting, so whale oil was increasingly harder to find

and more expensive. A fuel called *kerosene*—made out of oil shale or coal, and so often called *coal gas*—was also being used at this time. Kerosene could also be made from oil, and it was less expensive than coal gas. By the 1820s oil was beginning to replace both whale oil and kerosene from coal.

By the 1850s demand for oil was increasing. New inventions made kerosene produced from oil even less expensive than that produced from coal or oil shale. Demand for oil was also increasing for other reasons. The new industrial age by then sweeping much of the world created a rapidly growing mass of machines. Oil was needed to lubricate these machines, so the parts would move smoothly and easily (instead of "locking up" and overheating).

On August 27, 1859, Edwin L. Drake completed an oil well at Titusville in western Pennsylvania. Many have called it the first com-

Parts of what is now the major city of Los Angeles were once covered with oil derricks, as shown in this image dating from about 1905.

mercial oil well drilled in the United States and have hailed its completion as the birth of the American oil industry. Many others have pointed out that the first known producing North American oil well went into production in Kentucky in 1829.

Whether or not Drake's well was the first, his Titusville well came at a time when demand for oil was increasing in the United States. Many more oil wells soon began to be drilled in western Pennsylvania and then in many other parts of the country.

Existing supplies were more than enough to satisfy the need for oil during the 1800s. The tremendous boom in oil demand, use, and production came in the early 1900s, with the worldwide spread of the automobile, which used huge amounts of gasoline.

With the automobile age came many other massive oil needs. Oil was needed as fuel for ships, trains, planes, homes, and industries, and for all the other related uses that quickly developed. Then oil moved into the center of modern life, where it still is today.

The dune-covered deserts of Saudi Arabia were long thought to hold little of value to humans. However, today we know that under the sand lie some of the richest oil resources in the world.

Oil around the World

Oil is found throughout the world, on land and offshore in the shallow seas near today's continental shores. Offshore oil also often includes some of the large inland lakes and seas, such as the Black Sea and the Caspian Sea.

Many countries have producing oil wells and so-far untapped re- serves of oil. However, only a few countries have truly massive oil resources. Of these, only the United States and Russia are major indus- trial countries, using most of the oil they produce.

Most of the other oil-rich nations would, without their oil, be quite poor developing nations, like the great majority of the world's countries. Such oil-rich but not industrialized countries may be wealthy, but they are seldom very strong. This has often created major international problems, as stronger nations seek to dominate them and their oil.

The greatest known supplies of the world's oil are in a group of Middle Eastern nations located near the Persian Gulf, which are linked by their history and geography. Of these, Saudi Arabia has by far the greatest combination of current oil production and known oil reserves.

The region's other major oil-rich countries include Iran, Iraq, Kuwait, Abu Dhabi, and Qatar. Taken together, these Persian Gulf countries have the world's single greatest known body of oil resources.

The United States also has major oil resources, although these are not nearly as large as those of the Persian Gulf nations. The United States uses the oil it produces, for it is also by far the world's largest consumer of oil and other kinds of energy. Such energy is needed to power its massive industrial plants and its huge numbers of cars, homes,

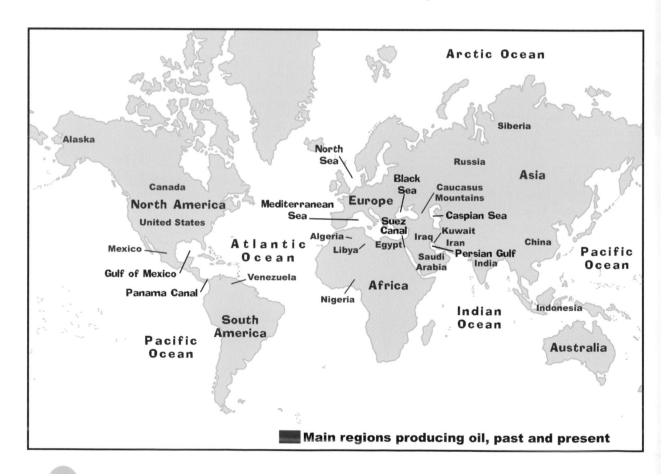

Main regions producing oil, past and present

Some offshore oil rigs lie very near the coastline, like this one in the Gulf of Mexico, with the skyline of Mobile, Alabama, in the background.

planes, and all kinds of other energy-consuming devices.

The United States also has substantial oil reserves offshore, much of it in the Arctic regions of Alaska. However, there is a long, major disagreement within the United States over whether oil drilling should be pursued in the Alaska wildlife preserves because of the potential for environmental damage (see p. 27).

Russia and the Central Asian countries that were formerly part of the Soviet Union are a third major oil-producing group of nations. Very large oil reserves have also been found offshore in the Caspian Sea. These were beginning to be tapped in the 21st century.

Drilling offshore under Europe's North Sea has been a major source of oil for several decades. Large, newly found oil fields have also been located offshore in Indonesia, and others are reported to exist in western China, Siberia, and off the east Asian coast.

Another North American country producing large amounts of oil is Mexico. It also has substantial oil reserves offshore in the Gulf of Mexico. In South America, Venezuela is the largest source of oil.

Some of the world's other oil-producing countries are Nigeria, Libya, Indonesia, Algeria, and China. However, none of them is a major producer. (China's actual production is not fully known, but is an estimate.)

These workers are putting into place the head of the drill for a new oil well. To cut through hard rock, the head is sometimes tipped with industrial-grade diamonds (not the quality that you would wear in jewelry).

Exploration and Drilling

In the early days of oil exploration, people usually searched for oil wells with a "hit or miss" method. Often they merely guessed that they might find oil near where it had previously been discovered. That was sometimes so, but this method resulted in far more bad guesses than successes. However, people prospecting for oil soon found better ways to find it, and experience in oil exploration grew fast.

In those early days many oil fields were found and put into production by oil companies. These companies soon came to dominate what grew to be the worldwide oil industry. However, a good many hopeful individuals and small companies also drilled for oil. Their wells were called *wildcat wells*. Whether big oil company wells or wildcat wells, those that failed to find oil were called *dry holes*.

Wells that succeeded often announced themselves with *gushers*. A gusher is a powerful jet of oil and gas that can go hundreds of feet high. It occurs when drillers hit a reservoir of oil in the ground, which is usually mixed with highly compressed natural gas under layers of rock (see p. 7). Once released, the gas bursts from the ground, carrying oil with it. As soon as possible after that, the gusher is *capped*—that is, covered—and its flow of valu-

able oil is captured. The oil can then be moved on to a refinery and later put to its huge number of uses (see p. 23).

For a long time the natural gas that came out of the ground with oil was regarded as only a nuisance to be burned off. Gas became a major energy source on its own after World War II ended in 1945. From then on it, too, was often carefully captured for its own many uses. However, most natural gas used as

In the early days of oil drilling, an oil strike was often announced with a huge burst of oil called a *gusher*, like this one in Texas in the early 1900s. The gusher would be capped as soon as possible so drillers could hold and then capture the valuable fluid.

When oil prospectors are developing possible new wells in an oil field, they construct a drilling rig, a tall structure that holds the drill that will bite deep into the ground to reach oil. This one was set up at the Elk Hills U.S. Naval Petroleum Reserve in California.

energy today comes not from oil reservoirs but rather from separate natural gas reservoirs.

Modern oil exploration uses far better tools than were available in oil's early days. By the early 1900s experts called *petroleum geologists* had developed instruments to help them determine the kinds of rock formations that exist underground. These helped them to find possible oil pools. Later they developed several kinds of instruments that could measure the movement of sound waves through rock formations and oil sources. These gave even more information about where oil might be found. With the help of modern computers, oil exploration has become even more effective.

The final step in oil exploration—as it was at the start of the oil industry—is the drilling of one or more test wells. The aim is to see whether oil is really there and, if so, to answer questions such as: How much oil is there? How deep is it? What kind is it? Is it worthwhile to go after it in a big way? This might include building hugely expensive pipelines to get the oil to refineries after it comes out of the ground (see p. 23).

This whole process can be very expensive. However, a new oil field is one of the most valuable sources of wealth in the world—so valuable that it quickly captures massive attention from big oil companies, governments, and concerned environmentalists.

Oil Drilling

Modern oil drilling is basically the same as it was in the early days of oil production. A big, high-powered drill with a very strong steel shaft and bit (head) is used to dig a hole deep into the ground, seeking oil. The drill is housed within a long pipe in a tall structure called a *derrick*. As the drill digs deeper into the ground, sections of pipe are added until the drill strikes oil—or the attempt is given up.

In the early days of oil exploration, some well holes were dug as little as 50 feet into the ground

Once oil has been discovered and an oil well has been drilled, pumps of various shapes, types, and sizes are used to bring the oil out of the ground. This one is a small type called a *jack pump*, nicknamed a *nodding monkey*, because the head rocks up and down as it works.

before they struck oil. Today many oil wells all over the world are 25,000 to 30,000 feet deep, and some go even deeper than that. In the early days of a new well or oil field, oil may gush out of wells. Later, however, it is pumped out. A variety of techniques may be used to make it easier to get the oil out of the ground.

Drilling for oil offshore is basically the same as drilling on land. However, the oil drilling and production rigs must be very different offshore.

A great deal of offshore drilling, especially in shallow waters, uses fixed platforms. These are platforms that solidly hold the oil drilling and production machinery.

Another way to handle drilling, especially in deeper water, is to do it from drill ships. These ships drill while floating on the surface of the water.

A third kind of offshore drilling operation is carried on from drilling platforms that are towed to where they are to be used. There they are set partially underwater, so that the weight of the water will make them more stable.

Oil rigs are often built near the shore and then towed out to where they will be settled onto the seabed like this offshore oil rig.

Much oil is carried by pipelines across vast distances. This is a section of the Alaska pipeline, which runs about 796 miles (1,284 kilometers) through wilderness to reach the southern coast at Valdez. It can carry 2 million barrels of crude oil a day.

From Oil Well to Refinery

Crude oil must be processed at a refinery into gasoline, heating oil, and many other products. To get to the refinery from the well, the oil must often travel many thousands of miles. Much oil and oil products travel by land, as when crude oil travels from Central Asia to Germany or from Texas to New York.

Today most oil travels on land through pipelines. Many small pipe-

Today much oil is carried around the world in huge tankers. The problem is that, if an accident occurs, the amount of oil spilled—and the danger to the environment—is enormous. This is the *Exxon Valdez*, which ran aground off Alaska in 1989, creating the largest oil spill in United States history.

lines travel from oil wells and oil fields to meet larger regional and transcontinental pipelines. That was not always so. Before World War II a great deal of oil traveled by railroad tank cars, tank trucks, and barges. After that war ended in 1945, a whole web of pipelines was built throughout the world.

A great deal of the world's oil is also transported by sea. In shallow coastal waters some oil is carried from offshore oil rigs by pipeline. However, most seaborne oil is carried in big, oceangoing oil tankers.

Some of these are huge super-tankers, so large that they cannot fit through the Panama Canal and the Suez Canal. As a result, they have to go all the way around South America and Africa (see p. 16).

Some of the world's worst environmental disasters have occurred while oil and oil products are being transported. These can result from pipeline breaks, huge oil spills, tankers breaking up during storms at sea, fires, and other such incidents (see p. 27).

The Oil Refinery

However it is transported, all crude oil ends its journey at an oil refinery. This is an industrial plant designed to process crude oil into many products. These include gasoline, jet fuel for aircraft, kerosene, diesel fuel, heating oils, and several other heavy fuels and fuel gases, as well as lubricants, asphalt, and petrochemicals of many kinds.

Crude oil arriving at a refinery does not immediately go into the refining process. Instead, it is stored before refining in large storage tanks or underground caves.

In the refining process crude oil goes first into a *fractioning tower* several hundred feet high. There it is heated until it reaches the boiling point of the lightest portions of the oil, which begin to boil at a little under 100 degrees Fahrenheit (about 38 degrees Celsius). At that temperature, the lighter parts of the boiling oil turn into vapor (a cloudy mist), which rises toward the top of the tower. These are then captured and cooled somewhat, so the vapor turns back into a liquid. The same process is repeated at ever-higher temperatures, so the different kinds of oil are separated out, one by one. These different kinds of oil are called *fractions*.

In tall *fractioning towers*, like this one in a California oil refinery, crude oil is boiled at ever-higher temperatures to separate out the different kinds of fuel in the oil. This process is called *fractional distillation*.

The lightest kinds of oils separated out by fractioning are several kinds of gases used for fuel, such as propane, methane, and butane, which are also used for making petrochemicals and light fuel oils.

Next in weight and requiring a higher boiling point is kerosene, used as heating oil, for light, and as part of other fuels.

Somewhat heavier is gasoline, which is by far the greatest single use of oil. Other kinds of fuels used in transportation follow, including diesel fuel. Then comes heavier oil for use in heating homes, industrial plants, and other structures.

The heaviest parts of the oil, among them asphalt, do not vaporize. Instead, they sink to the bottom of the tower.

This whole process is called *fractional distillation*. It is basically the same kind of distillation process that has been used to clean and purify many kinds of substances for thousands of years.

A further process called *cracking* continues refining the fuel oil fractions produced by distillation. The chemical structures of these fractions are changed into even lighter fuels, especially gasoline.

Further still in the refining process, distilled and cracked fractions are chemically changed even more. This is done so that they can be made into thousands of oil-based and petrochemical-based products.

Because oil is so important to our modern life, governments hold large amounts of it in reserve. Some is stored underground, as here in Texas. Arriving or leaving from tankers or pipelines, oil is pumped into and out of the site, with the pumping flow monitored by meters, as shown here.

Oil spills that wash up on coastlines are sometimes so heavy that clean-up workers scoop up the oil with shovels and carry it away in bags, as above in Newport Beach, California, in 1990. Many animals and plants are damaged in the water and on land, like this oil-soaked bird (right) that was killed on the Saudi Arabian coast after the massive Persian Gulf oil spill in 1991.

Oil—Dangers and Disasters

Oil is a great and very necessary treasure. Yet at the same time, it presents large and worldwide dangers to the environment. Oil can very quickly cause *pollution*—that is, it can make the environment harmful to living things, poisoning or even killing animals and plants.

Probably the largest source of oil-caused pollution is from "normal" oil leaks and spills. These everyday events occur throughout all the processes of finding, drilling, producing, transporting, and processing petroleum.

Storage tanks can also leak into

Massive oil spills get an enormous amount of attention. However, far more oil goes into the environment from everyday spills wherever oil is found, transported, or used, as here in a small oil well in Texas.

the surrounding ground. Even small continuing leaks, from any source, can pollute wide areas, including underground water supplies.

Sometimes the environment is endangered by huge oil leaks. These can and sometimes do occur during drilling for oil and later oil production. Massive oil leaks have occurred at offshore oil rigs, including many highly polluting oil fires.

The largest oil spill on record took place in 1979. That was when the Mexican Ixtoc I well blew up in the Gulf of Mexico, releasing 600,000 tons of oil.

Major accidents can also happen while oil is being transported from oil wells to the refineries that turn oil into its basic products (see p. 23). Pipeline breaks and leaks on land can threaten plant and animal life. Such hazards are a major concern when oil pipelines are intended to go through wilderness areas.

Some of the most disastrous oil spills have occurred at sea or in other waterways. Two of the worst oil disasters resulted when tankers ran aground. In 1978 the super-tanker *Amoco Cadiz* spilled 226,000 tons of oil into the sea, fouling some 200 miles of coastline in France's Brittany region. In 1989 the *Exxon Valdez*, carrying oil from the sea end of the Alaska pipeline, spilled 37,000 tons of oil into the sea off Valdez, Alaska. The worst oil spill in American history, that accident killed at least 50,000 birds and a great deal of other wildlife and con-

taminated at least 1,100 miles of Alaska shoreline.

Oil disasters can also occur during war. Some are accidental, but others are deliberate. In 1991, during the Persian Gulf War, Iraqi forces released at least 70,000 tons of oil from their Sea Island Terminal into the Persian Gulf. Even worse, they set fire to an estimated 650 Kuwaiti oil wells. This created a huge cloud of oil smoke that spread from several Middle Eastern countries into much of southwest Asia. These actions also polluted thousands of miles of coastline and killed a huge number of seabirds, fish, and other wildlife.

During the Persian Gulf War, Iraqi forces attacked hundreds of Kuwaiti oil installations, setting many aflame, such as this offshore oil rig. Black, oily smoke and the oil itself greatly damaged the environment.

29

Words to Know

asphalt One of the heaviest, thickest forms of OIL, often used on road surfaces.

barrel A measure of the volume of OIL. One barrel of oil most commonly equals 42 gallons.

cracking The separation of fuel oil fractions into even lighter fuels, by changing their chemical structures (see FRACTIONAL DISTILLATION).

crude oil: See OIL.

declining resource A natural resource, such as OIL or coal, that is being used up.

desulfurization plant An industrial plant that removes sulfur from SOUR CRUDE oil.

dry holes OIL wells that have been drilled without finding oil.

fossil fuels Fuels, like OIL and coal, made of ancient plant matter buried for millions of years under layers of SEDIMENTARY ROCK. Heat, pressure, and chemical change all combine to change the buried matter into oil.

fraction: See FRACTIONAL DISTILLATION.

fractional distillation The cleaning and separation of CRUDE OIL into several kinds of oil, called *fractions*. This takes place in a *fractioning tower* several hundred feet high, where oil is heated, boiled, vaporized, and cooled, separating the lighter kinds of oil from the heavier kinds.

gusher A powerful jet of OIL mixed with gas that can go hundreds of feet high, when oil drillers hit a reservoir of oil, releasing both gas and oil.

hydrocarbon A large family of chemicals, made of the elements hydrogen and carbon. PETROCHEMICALS, which are hydrocarbons derived from petroleum, are at the center of the modern chemical industry.

offshore drilling Drilling for OIL into land covered by water, as in shallow coastal waters or in deeper waters farther out.

oil (petroleum) A kind of FOSSIL FUEL, made mainly of HYDROCARBONS and including varying amounts of oxygen, nitrogen, and sulfur. In its natural state it is called *crude oil*.

oil refinery An industrial plant that exists to process crude OIL into several kinds of oil that, in the end, are used to make thousands of products.

oil shale A kind of rock containing a heavy OIL that is much like petroleum (see OIL) but is not thought to be true petroleum.

oil spill The accidental release of a substantial quantity of OIL into the environment. Some oil spills, as from supertankers and big pipelines, have become major environmental disasters. Even smaller oil spills can cause substantial damage.

oil tanker A ship that carries oil. Some large *supertankers* are so big that they cannot pass through the Panama or Suez Canals.

petrochemical A chemical derived from petroleum (see OIL); a kind of HYDROCARBON.

petroleum: See OIL.

pipeline A pipe carrying quantities of oil, or any other liquid or gas, from an oil well or storage tank to a larger pipeline or a refinery.

pour point The temperature at which a kind of OIL can be poured.

sediment Soil and other natural materials that have settled to the bottom of a body of water, such as a flowing stream.

sedimentary rock A kind of rock that was originally SEDIMENT but over many millions of years has turned into solid rock.

sour crude OIL containing large amounts of sulfur.

sweetened oil OIL that was originally SOUR CRUDE but has had most of the sulfur removed.

tank car A railroad car that carries OIL or any other liquids.

tar sands A kind of sand containing heavy OIL.

test well An exploratory OIL well, dug to see if oil really is there and how much it might cost to get it out of the ground.

viscosity How freely OIL flows, primarily a matter of thickness.

wildcat well A kind of OIL well, drilled in hope of finding oil by an independent driller or small company.

On the Internet

The Internet has many interesting sites about oil. The site addresses often change, so the best way to find current addresses is to go to a search site, such as www.yahoo.com. Type in a word or phrase, such as "oil" or "petroleum."

As this book was being written, websites about oil included:

http://www.fe.doe.gov
Fossil Energy website, which includes materials for students, including a glossary; part of the U.S. Department of Energy:
http://www.energy.gov/

http://www.classroom-energy.org
An online resource for students and teachers from the American Petroleum Institute, which also offers news and consumer information about oil and environmental concerns at:
http://api-ec.api.org/newsplashpage/index.cfm

http://www.nsta.org/energy/
National Science Teachers Association resources on energy matters.

http://www.pcf.ab.ca/
Petroleum Communication Foundation, a Canadian website offering a glossary of oil-related terms, links, and other information.

In Print

Your local library system will have various books on oil. The following is just a sampling of them.

Berger, Bill D., and Kenneth E. Anderson. *Modern Petroleum*. Tulsa, OK: Pennwell, 1981.

Blashfield, Jean F., and Wallace B. Black. *Oil Spills*. Chicago: Children's Press, 1991.

Cook, Earl. *Man, Energy, Society*. San Francisco: W. H. Freeman, 1976.

Cranfield, John, and David Buckman. *Oil*. Hove, Sussex, UK: Priory Press, 1976.

Franck, Irene M., and David M. Brownstone. *The Green Encyclopedia*. New York: Prentice-Hall, 1992.

Landes, Kenneth. *Petroleum Geology*. Huntington, NY: Robert E. Krieger, 1976.

Nye, Donald E. *Consuming Power*. Cambridge, MA: MIT Press, 1999.

Pampe, William R. *Petroleum*. Hillside, NJ: Enslow, 1984.

Van Nostrand's Scientific Encyclopedia, 8th ed., 2 vols. Douglas M. Considine and Glenn D. Considine, eds. New York: Van Nostrand Reinhold, 1995.

Waddams, A. Lawrence. *Chemicals from Petroleum*. New York: Wiley, 1971.

Index